FISH in LAKES and RIVERS

By

John Hodgson

ISBN: 9798645567125

Over and over all about some fish are close to each other. While some swim for recreation in formation.

John Hodgson

Fish swim in formation to develop relationships from within so they get to know each other's fin.

The fish understand each other so they can make fun and grow strong. Within their network the fish belong.

John Hodgson

Fish will mingle and stay their territory. For their lives that make them rich.

With nutrients for all the fish. The fish learn to eat from the others.

John Hodgson

Each fish swims fast within the rivers
with no bothers.

Their life is transformed with all their energy. That they enjoy with their others.

John Hodgson

With direction fish swim from the river and away. At which they just know to swim to the bay.

Into the lake and out of the bay. The fish learn to stay. Into the lake and out of the bay.

John Hodgson

In the lake many fish join a school.
Each fish belonging in the pool.

As the fish swim diligently. The fish have to be in the pool.

John Hodgson

So, they learn to be no fool and stay
in the pool.

As fish swim close to the shore they see the sunlight and know when to strike.

John Hodgson

The food that exists when you're a pike.

Even the fish know the date. From the water's temperature that is. The season of the weather and all is at stake.

John Hodgson

As the water cools some of the
fish like to swim like a pike.

Every time a fish swims, it has to use its fins, to navigate, over and over to win with its fin.

John Hodgson

In the school of fish, a fish's life is about being proud. So, they can to live and flourish all around.

In the school the fish have importance. To respect each other with accordance.

John Hodgson

Fish swimming all around. They learn to hunt and roam around.

To find food and not to intrude. On others that are so far.

From each other distance. So,
each fish can find their existence.

Within the fish school or pool. The fish have to adapt. So, each can have, a life of act.

John Hodgson

All the fish have their days, where
they can have praise.

From the other fish they know so, all fish can be fish and develop and grow.

John Hodgson

Fish swim with each other. In a pool
or a school.

Fish partake in what they need to succeed. In a pool or in a school.

John Hodgson

The water in the lake can be great. For fish to swim and swim alike. To keep and give to each other. To provide food with their hunger.

As the fish swim they find food near the wake in a lake.

John Hodgson

When the fish find the wake, they participate to receive food they found. Now isn't that profound.

When the fish are all fed, they leave the wake and swim into the greater lake.

John Hodgson

Schools of fish gravitating in the
water so great. With the current
they migrate.

In their groups at their whim.
They make fun as they swim.

John Hodgson

Swimming everywhere ever so fast.
They have a blast.

In the lake away from the wake is where they swim so awake.

John Hodgson

Some swimming away from at each
other, at no bother. Others
swimming around and gather.

Swimming with the others a fish makes a wish. For some to swim on a whim.

John Hodgson

Each fish grants their fun. Swimming and swimming around everyone.

The fish become great fish to list. A new chapter the fish to exist.

John Hodgson

As the fish pertain to swim ever so swift. They become a fish's fish.

Travelling in the lake so rich, with all the fish, that was the wish.

John Hodgson

To have all the fun under the sun
and with the waters swish. With
everyone everywhere with all the
other fish.

So, the fish made all their fun. In the sun and water without a bother.

John Hodgson

As the sunshine led the fish to lead.
The fun was with all and all to see.
The day was great and very happy.

The fish have a good delight.
Finding their food in the morning
light.

John Hodgson

Jumping up out of the water. To
catch the food that matter.

To feed themselves and all to eat.

John Hodgson

The water is warmer near the shore.
The fish like this and eat more and
more.

Of the food they engage with a chore.

John Hodgson

Fish that are smart will last the journeys chart.

Of the route they embark upon. In the lakes and rivers that they encounter.

John Hodgson

Throughout their days they find
their fun in the lakes and rivers with
everyone.

The fish find what they need as nature so intended. So, fish will swim and swim.

John Hodgson

In the lakes and rivers is where the fish are.

To find the fish near or from afar.

John Hodgson

The fish will be there in the lake or
river.

So, to see them swim near you will have to be clever.

THE END

www.ingramcontent.com/pod-product-compliance
Lightning Source LLC
Chambersburg PA
CBHW050700250726
48662CB00002B/776